Understanding and Healing the Inner Child

How to recognize unresolved conflicts within yourself, get in touch with your inner child, strengthen and heal it to finally blossom in full vitality

Julia Wiederspohn

CONTENT

What you can expect in this book

Are you said to be a perfectionist? Are you extremely addicted to harmony, do you react to certain conflicts in your relationship with iciness or blind rage? Do you often want to please others until you feel exhausted, does it even go as far as extreme self-sacrifice? Are there always similar situations in which you react unusually emotionally?

These could all be indications that you have suffered from trauma wounds in your childhood that are still waiting to be healed. I would like to invite you on a journey through time. A journey into your past. "Back to the future" would be a fitting motto for this journey, because what you experienced in your earliest child-hood has a direct influence on your behavior in the present.

You will learn what the model of the inner child is all about and gain insights that will enable you to track down your individual behavioral patterns that originate as a reaction to experiences in early childhood and to consciously change them. Are you one of those people who keep attracting the same conflicts, people or situations into your life? Now you have a great opportunity to recognize and stop these negative cycles.

You will learn a lot about yourself on this journey, understand your own emotions better, and it will reveal to you what is really the message behind your behavior patterns. Know that each of us has an inner child, so understanding this part of a person's psyche will provide you with a deeper understanding of yourself and others, and improve your interpersonal relationships. This child in all of us wants to be noticed! It will - like a small child - tug and whine at you until you give it attention and meet its needs. Then - in all areas of life - peace can come.

The fun factor on this very personal journey for you will definitely not be neglected! You will also learn how to integrate the positive feelings you felt as a child into everyday life. When was the last time you were carefree and enthusiastic about something? Learn to see things with the eyes of a child again, full of enthusiasm and curiosity.

You can expect a selection of methods to get in touch with your inner child and numerous practical examples of when and why your inner child comes out, even though you are not aware of it. By embracing the child within you, a whole new perspective on your life may open up; the pursuit of ideals that are otherwise important to you will suddenly no longer be appropriate and can be replaced by something else, more wholesome. Your relationships will improve and in the future you can lead a healthier life through more self-love and acceptance. In the future, your partner or work colleague may be amazed to find you reacting calmly in situations where you used to quickly go off into the deep end.

The exercises you will learn in this book can be done all by yourself or with your partner or a good friend. You will learn in a playful way that a child is active in each of us, and you will get to know yourself or each other in a way that strengthens the intimate bond with each other.

At the end of the journey, you may feel well prepared for the next small or large crisis of everyday life, because the situations that used to emotionally wear you down can now be avoided with ease. Are you ready?

The model of the inner child

EARLY CHILDHOOD IMPRINTING AND THERAPEUTIC APPROACHES

In the first weeks of life, an infant still perceives itself as a perfect unit with its mother; from the third month, the exciting learning process of life begins. Initially, infant connect experiences that associate his behavior with a particular outcomes, such as crying with the intake of food or reaching for an object when it is offered. Reactions of the mother are perceived as a mirror and the infant's own body perception slowly develops. At the beginning of the second year of life, the toddler develops his own will and experiences limits for the first time, which end in tears and disappointment when they are set. At the end of the second year of life, we recognize our reflection in the mirror as our own "I". Our independence begins here. From the third year of life, a child establishes a connection between cause and effect, but sees the cause of a praise, a rebuke, a ban or a scolding in himself.

Innocent and completely in the hands of parents, we as infants have only these basic needs: nutrition, health, sleep, safety, love, acceptance and security. It is during the first years of life between 0 and 6 that positive and negative experiences are unconsciously stored for the future - on our hard drive. Here the foundation is laid for our later development and learning ability, these are equal to the later social skills of each person.

The painful experiences in early childhood have triggered fears or resistance to further experiences in the young child, and he or she has learned protective and defensive mechanisms to cope with the experiences. Furthermore, as young children we learned how to behave to avoid these situations. In the process, our perception may have been suppressed or we may have distrusted our feelings, denied them or considered them to be wrong and pretensive.

Every child has the desire to be loved by its parents, and if in the course of its personal development, it repeatedly experiences rejection, punishment or coldness on the part of its caregivers, the need is gradually suppressed. This is an unconscious protective function in the brain, according to brain researcher Gerald Hüther. The neurologist explains that this mechanism, called "coherence," is essential so that the brain, and inevitably the whole person, uses the least amount of energy. This state is achieved when all neurological and biological processes fit together optimally. If a conflict arises between the child's need for recognition and the parent's rejection, then the coherence is disturbed and this state very quickly becomes imbalanced because the brain's neurons begin to fire in an uncoordinated manner. This results in discomfort and we look for a solution. When the solution is found, the brain chemistry becomes more coherent again and we feel better. For this reason, the small child willingly gives up its needs. According to Gerald Hüther, there is then another circumstance that involuntarily rewards this neurological function: the praise of the parents because the child is good.

He goes on to say that it is precisely these neurological processes that ensure that we fit in well with family and society. He concludes that, for example, a good school degree is not necessarily an indicator of intelligence and diligence, but of good adaptability. The more the brain gets involved in suppressing needs and personality traits, the more adaptable a person is.

The researcher is convinced that one is never really happy in this state, because the constantly burgeoning needs are pushed away with a high energy expenditure in the brain. Those affected always continue to adapt to the external circumstances of life, fit in everywhere and have no individual development. They have lost important qualities such as zest for life, spontaneity and passion. The good news is that the brain is rebuildable throughout life and it is never too late to break free from learned patterns of behavior and feelings. This requires getting back in touch with our needs and personality traits. Brain research describes this ability as "neuroplasticity".

In psychotherapy, since the 1990s, one considers the inner child as a model for the individual experiences of childhood, i.e. a bundle of feelings, memories and experiences. Feelings such as joy, pain, happiness, sadness, intuition, curiosity, abandonment, loneliness, fear and anger are experienced by the young child, but due to the still missing self-reflection of an adult consciousness, they are later transformed into dysfunctional and unhealthy patterns of belief and life.

In various psychotherapeutic approaches, work with the inner child is used to heal psychological wounds and traumas of childhood, to find more self-love, self-confidence and overall a healthier way of dealing with oneself. A two-part perspective is consciously adopted, that of the observing, adult and reflected consciousness and that of the experiencing little inner child. In this way, connections can be made by bringing the causal connection out of the unconscious state into consciousness, understood and accepted, illuminated and healed.

The integration of negative past experiences and dissolution of burdening behavior patterns are by no means new. As a fixed component in psychotherapeutic work, in alternative-spiritual healing circles for trauma resolution or seminars for personality development and coaching, this principle has many siblings, e.g. the integration of the "shadow ego", family constellations according to Bert Hellinger, the Hawaiian forgiveness prayer, Ho'Opoono, NLP, etc.

In principle, it is always about letting go of the pain from the past and healing the feelings associated with it. The concept of the inner child is not only attracting attention in the Western world through many guidebooks and seminars, but is also, for example, an integral part of Buddhism for a happier life.

HOW DO I RECOGNIZE IF I CARRY UNRESOLVED CONFLICTS FROM CHILDHOOD?

Well, I can reassure you no childhood is perfect, writes Stefanie Stahl in her bestseller "The Child in You Must Find Home." Neither are there perfect parents nor the perfect childhood. So for now, we should be relaxed about working with the inner child, because we have all experienced conflict. However, there is some evidence to suggest that unhealthy behaviors have manifested because of the early childhood experience:

1. Control constraint
2. Lack of empathy and empathy for the other person, coldness in the partnership, "stonewalling" or "shutting down" during conflicts.
3. Problems in dealing with authority figures
4. Strong rebellion against imposed social, societal, family or partnership rules of the game.

5. Harmony addiction (including self-abandonment, exhaustion, depression, burn-out)

6. Fear of loss (e.g., creating dependencies and remaining in unhealthy relationships, submissiveness).

7. Taking on a victim role (e.g. grumbling, nagging, complaining)

8. Lack of willingness to compromise (e.g. always "looking for the fly in the ointment", being a spoilsport)

9. Perfectionism (e.g., no self-awareness of one's own limits, physical and mental expenditure, increased discipline, e.g., in sports, nutrition, at work, self-hardness).

10. Lack of self-love (e.g. rejection of one's own body, beauty mania)

11. Addictive behavior (alcohol, drugs, etc.)

12. Severe mood swings, inappropriate emotional outbursts.

13. Lack of confidence in self and others (e.g., jealousy, control, feelings of inferiority)

14. Excessive ego-centeredness (e.g., strong desire to always see one's own needs met, if necessary by always creating new diseases or lies).

The degree of stress and whether it is accompanied by suffering varies greatly from person to person. Since we all strive for more serenity, relaxation and health, we should take a closer look, because stress and conflicts lead to undesirable side effects in the long run.

Even feelings in everyday situations that seem subtle at first glance are worth taking a closer look at. For example, if you are angry with your boss all weekend because he sent you a task half an hour before closing time on Friday, so you can't enjoy your free time and go to the office in a bad mood on Monday. Or you have been looking forward to a planned outing or event for some time and on the day itself you are not in the mood, perhaps you have psychosomatic symptoms of illness such as back pain or headaches. An argument with your partner escalates, the so-called mosquito turns into an elephant. A stranger on the street criticizes you because of a trifle and inside, you glow with anger and it hangs onto you for a long time.

SHADOW AND SUN CHILD

The child part of our personality is basically seen in two parts in therapeutic work. The child in us, which was loved, accepted and accepted by the parents, is often called "sun child" or also "happy child". All positive experiences and experienced feelings are assigned to the "sun child" and express themselves especially through personality traits such as joy, spontaneity, openness, curiosity, enthusiasm, sense of responsibility, humor, empathy.

In contrast to the "Sun Child," the "Shadow Child" has experienced rejection, been ignored, treated with severity, felt a lack of love, or been abandoned. The negative feelings and experiences are assigned to the "Shadow Child" or the "Unhappy Child". Personality traits such as sadness, frustration, anger, envy, jealousy, shame, etc. show up as examples.

The symbolic distinction between the happy, carefree and fun-loving child and the sad, lonely and rejected child serves to simplify and assign negative and positive beliefs and can be used independently for personal work with the inner child.

It is important that you internalize that your subconscious mind strives throughout your life to relive the painful and negative experiences that were not processed as a child and have left a permanent mark on you. These situations, issues, circumstances and people with the corresponding "matching" character-istics are presented to you and unconsciously invited into your life by you until you find a (re)solution. You do this not consciously to continue experiencing these negative feelings or to lick your wounds, but to find a cure, a happy ending. Your inner child shows you a path of healing, of conflict resolution, which often leads through the pain. But it also helps you realize that it is time to end unhealthy cycles.

Examples from practice

THE INNER CHILD IN THE PARTNERSHIP

The partner we choose depends on several factors, yet the inner child is often the driving force, the motor in the choice for the life partner, and also for friends or lovers. The inner child seeks and finds its parents in these partnerships, couple therapists agree. What we were denied as a child, what we did not receive then, the unconscious part in us now hopes to get. Therefore, it is not surprising that we are often attracted to people who are similar to our father or mother. These can be external as well as internal characteristics.

However, there is also the exact opposite: if the behavior of the parents was strongly rejected, then we look for a person who embodies the exact opposite of the parents behavior at first sight. It may well happen that after the initial infatuation phase, it is recognized that the partner then turns into a parent in terms of behavior after all, and the disappointment about this is understandably great.

How can I tell that the inner child is involved in choosing a partner?

- We always end up with partners who are similarly unfaithful, emotionally hypothermic, quick-tempered, jealous, controlling, etc. (just as one of our parents was).
- We experience our parents' marriage vicariously in our marriage or relationship. The partner takes the position of a parent in his behavior and we automatically transform into the other parent. ("Yet I never wanted to become like my mother .../my father ...").
- We take on the responsibility in a partnership but actually long for a strong shoulder, want to let go and experience support. (This might sound familiar to you if you were left to your own devices too early as a child or were responsible for your siblings).

- A partner is chosen because they shower us with attention and care, perhaps controls or manipulates or bullies us (as father or mother did).
- The partner rejects us, ignores us, leaves us alone, does not allow closeness (e.g. if the mother left us physically or emotionally alone too early or the father punished us with ignorance when we misbehaved).
- We never come first for the partner (this is often the case with siblings, when the parents gave more attention to the sibling).

When we fall in love with another person, a comprehensive healing of the inner child takes place on both sides, because you feel completely accepted by the other person, you experience unconditional love and security and the (sun) child in you experiences the repressed feelings of an intact, happy child. When we are in love, we can pull out trees, nothing brings us out of balance, we feel happiness, joy of life, spontaneity, suddenly we see everything through rose-colored glasses, the sky hangs full of violins. We are completely connected with ourselves. We see our heart person as perfect and perfect, because we are also whole and perfect in ourselves in this phase.

When we are in love, our brain releases more neurotransmitters that make us happy, because they have a direct influence on the perception of feelings and stimulate the affected brain areas. What is interesting here is that these areas also belong to the reward system of the neurological structure.

The phase of infatuation is not compared to an intoxication for nothing, because strictly speaking, we are under the influence of the drug dopamine. In order for the body to adapt to this exceptional situation, the stress hormone adrenaline is produced, along with several other messenger substances. This cocktail of chemical compounds makes us experience a phase of infatuation between two weeks and two years. Strictly speaking, it means that when you fall in love, you expose your body to a permanent stress situation. This state consumes a lot of resources energetically and physically and therefore cannot be sustained in the long term.

There comes a time when the brain reduces the release of these messenger substances and slowly but surely turns off our supply. This is a protective mechanism to bring our biological system back into balance. Now it is time to stabilize the bond with your partner. The first conflicts are brewing, disappointments are happening and with them emotional injuries again, which are similar to those we were exposed to in childhood.

Situation: Sabine comes home from work, is upset and angry about her boss and impulsively tells her boyfriend Arno about her experience in a raised, loud voice and gives vent to her rage. The louder Sabine talks herself into a rage, the less Arno reacts. When there is no reaction from him, she asks him indignantly, "Are you listening to me at all?" to which he replies, "Of course, you've been talking about nothing else for twenty minutes." Sabine is triggered and accuses her boyfriend of not being interested in her and of only ever caring about himself anyway. She gets louder and louder and Arno unceremoniously gets up and goes into the garage to escape the situation. Sabine is horrified, runs after him and bites into his calf like a terrier, provoking him - getting louder and louder - to get a reaction. Arno doesn't react at all until he explodes or leaves the house altogether.

Here it is not two adults arguing with each other, but five-year-old Sabine and six-year-old Arno. Sabine was often ignored by her mother or her needs were simply ignored and she felt that she was not taken seriously as a child. Arno's father was choleric and often yelled and screamed, Arno learned to escape from this situation, which was unbearable for him, only by running away. As a child he saw in himself as the cause of his father's anger.

Situation: Ute is upset because her husband Kurt has a habit of frequently leaving his socks lying around and she explodes when he comes home after work and is already taking off his work clothes in the hallway. Ute asks him if she is just his maid and that she is always cleaning up after him and is not his mother. Kurt is tired and exhausted and is met by his "nagging" wife and soon it doesn't stop at socks or work clothes on the floor. Kurt reproaches Ute for how long his day was and that she wants to make his end of the day hell and that he can't do anything right for her anyway. Again, this is really a conflict between little Ute and little Kurt. Ute was often scolded and punished when she was untidy. Her parents were very particular about cleanliness and order and only praised her when she did her household chores, which were expected of her. As a child, little Kurt was often criticized by his mother, who did not speak well of him. Recognition and praise were denied him.

Situation: Linda had an appointment at a car repair shop and tells her boyfriend, crying, that they had ripped her off mercilessly, that they had treated her unfriendly and that as a woman she would not be taken seriously there anyway. Her boyfriend Marco asks her more ironically than indignantly what she would expect of him, whether he should call there or drive right by? A heated argument develops, in which Linda accuses Marco of never standing up for her and of having bad luck in life, etc. Marco feels unjustly criticized by Marco. Marco feels unjustly criticized and lists all the things he does for Linda and that she is a whiner and shouldn't make such a fuss. Linda grew up as a child without a mother and only received increased undivided attention from her father, who had to take care of her and her three siblings, when she was helpless and crying. She was expected to be independent early on, and taking on a victim role often got her the attention she wanted from her father. Marco's mother, on the other hand, suffered from a chronic illness that almost exclusively determined everyday family life. Marco had to take care of his siblings and mother early on, who often sank into self-pity and did not perceive the needs of the children.

Situation: Kerstin is in a relationship with the choleric and pathologically jealous Stefan. Stefan checks Kerstin's cell phone, opens her mail, and regularly makes a scene accusing her of infidelity. Kerstin suffers greatly from this accusations, but is unable to free herself from this toxic relationship. She tries to do everything right for him and fulfills all the demands Stefan makes of her because she wants to make him happy. In her last relationship, Kerstin got involved with an alcoholic man, this relationship was also very bad for her and yet she was unable to separate from this man for a long time.

Kerstin's parents divorced when Kerstin was two years old. She grew up with her mother and subsequently broke off contact with her father. The trauma of losing her father runs deep, so she never wants to feel lonely, alone or abandoned again. Stefan was neglected by his parents and did not receive any appreciation, he was often verbally abused. He eventually grew up with his grandparents. He has developed an inferior self-esteem, always fears the infidelity of his partner, because he feels he is worth nothing.

Situation: Marion comes home full of enthusiasm - half an hour late - her joy is written all over her face because she has won two tickets for an outdoor adventure and cheers for her husband Ernst. He, however, is busy with his cell phone and whispers to her that he still has work to do and how important the new order is. Marion is disappointed and sadly withdraws. Marion grew up with a sister.

The parents' attention was often focused on the sibling, Marion often felt ignored and the impression was formed in her that she received less love and recognition than her sister. Ernst was brought up very dutifully and often received praise and recognition when an achievement was made. Time to play and free space did not have much room or priority. Marion's inner child wants to rejoice and share enthusiasm with her partner, but since Ernst does not respond as enthusiastically as she had hoped, she feels set back and ignored. Ernst, however, wants to fulfill his duties before he allows himself any freedom, and he is annoyed by the lack of punctuality, because for him it is a sign of disinterest. His father often promised to be present at school plays or sporting events and was often much too late and missed his son's school activities.

Based on the examples, you may now have gotten an idea of how the inner child significantly influences any conflict, crisis, potential dispute in a relationship.

In most cases, it is the little children in you and your partner who come into conflict with each other. They push, kick, punch, scold, break toys, react stubbornly, withdraw when insulted or stick out their tongues at each other. With this realization, you have already made the first progress toward improvement. It doesn't matter if your partner knows about his inner child and is aware of it. When you deal with and heal your inner child, you defuse all emotionally charged situations through your behavior and changed communication. You have recognized and made peace with your negative beliefs and imprints that are causing you pain, and from a healed state you can look at the situation in a completely different way.

In other words, you now evaluate the situation from an adult consciousness and whether your partner has left his dishes on the kitchen table or has done something else, which usually disappointed you or made you boil with anger, is perceived by you as a neutral situation - completely value-free - and in the best case taken quite calmly. Our world view and our imprints give all situations their spice. This also explains the fact that the same situations cause different reactions in different people. The husband's unpolished shoes can cause shame and insults in the first wife at Sunday brunch, but the second wife doesn't care at all, she doesn't even notice it.

Once you have changed the perspective, you can formulate your wishes and hopes clearly and directly. If Sabine had noticed how she was talking herself into a rage in the first example, she could have sent Arno ahead: "I'm sorry that I'm so upset now, but I have to let off some anger first until I can calm down. It has nothing to do with you! It would be nice if you would just listen to me and tell me what you would have done in my situation." Arno would not have felt guilty and would not have fled, the situation would have been defused.

In the second example, Ute could have said, for example, "You know, Kurt, I know you've had a long day and you're looking forward to the shower. But it's not my job to put your things away. You'd be helping me a lot if you'd put them in the linen chest yourself." With a wink, she could have added, "And in the future, if I find another pair of your socks under the sofa, they go in the trash." Sometimes even a humorous or sarcastic remark conveys an important message. Ute showed her husband appreciation and at the same time openly expressed her wishes.

In our third example, Linda could have expressed how helpless and run over she felt in this situation and how nice it would have been if Marco had been there, because he could negotiate much better since he knew his way around the industry. He would certainly have replied that he would accompany her to such appointments in the future.

In the next example, Kerstin has realized that her inner child has not coped with the loss of her father and feels panic when it comes to being alone. She therefore remains in unhealthy relationships or exposes herself to dependencies. By healing her personal trauma, she finds the self-awareness and confidence to end the relationship and the realization to replace "the emptiness" of not having a partner with other positive things.

In the last example, a simple apology for being late would have led directly to Ernst saying, "Yeah great! I'm looking forward to it! I still have to take care of this assignment, but when I'm done, we can plan our trip, okay?" If Marion had additionally expressed her hope that Ernst would also be as excited as she was, both parties in this situation would have been satisfied by the compromise.

Changing your perspective requires a little practice and attention and may not be successful right away. It is also possible that - even though you are working with your inner child - you will still fall back into old patterns of behavior and communication. Be patient with yourself. No master has fallen from the sky and some imprints from the past are deeper than others. There will be life issues that you can easily get a grip on, while others may seem to be unconquerable, some can never be completely disempowered. Step by step, you'll become more relaxed and at ease, noticing that a much deeper understanding of each other develops, your relationship improves significantly, and you're rewarded with a happy and fulfilling bond in the long run. And in the end, you simply feel better because you allow yourself to be who you are and call a spade a spade. You have better control over your emotions, are no longer a victim of unconsciously running programs, and can proactively intervene when a conflict threatens to get out of hand.

THE INNER CHILD AT WORK

As a reminder, your inner child accompanies you everywhere, because it is part of your personality. That it makes itself felt in the workplace is quite likely, because we live in a society that defines itself by performance and status. We learned very early to function, to achieve, to deny our desires instead of engaging in things that bring us joy (but may not provide us with life's income). We have learned in our society to elbow out, to assert ourselves, to play by rules that are not ours. We adapt because we believe we are at the bottom of the food chain. Very early on, we learned how reprisals, punishment, and restrictions follow if we don't "play along." We may accept daily hierarchies that do not value us, and spend a life time doing many virtual things that we cannot grasp and immediately experience no positive outcome.

It is worth looking very closely at what your inner child wants from your workplace and whether these needs are largely being met. If this is not the case, you should start healing your inner child quickly! I am certainly not telling you anything new when I point out that in the long run many illnesses have their origin in an unhealthy and unhappy working relationship.

The following workplace behaviors may indicate conflict in your shadow child:

- You can't say no, often feel overwhelmed because you're taking on more work than you can handle in terms of time or staff.

- You want to do everything yourself and find it hard to ask for help because you interpret it as failure if you ask for support.

- You don't listen to your body's signals, you may even go to work sick because you fear letting colleagues down or that people may equate your absence with weakness or secretly label you a malingerer.

- You accept conditions at work that are inwardly repugnant to you for fear of losing the job.

- You always try to deliver better results than your colleagues, following the motto higher, faster, further, to the point of self-sacrifice and mental and physical exhaustion.

- You change jobs frequently, feel like a victim of recurring circumstances.

- You do not recognize authority and openly or covertly rebel against people higher up in your hierarchy.

- As a supervisor, you have no empathy for your employees.

> • It is always the same colleague whom you would like to vaporize with a laser gun because he/she ... (here you are welcome to add what upsets you :-)).
> • You react to criticism with disproportionate sensitivity or defensiveness.

Please also be aware here that the inner child also comes into play in your colleagues and superiors. In principle, the same unconscious behavioral patterns come into play here as in all interpersonal relationships and can thus lead to stress at work if, for example, we behave inappropriately because we feel unfairly treated or are unable to deal with criticism. Perhaps your boss is a choleric person and reacts extremely impulsively, causing you to regularly shout at each other on the shop floor? In some situations, perhaps you ignore instructions "from above" and/or do just the opposite? Do you try to get other colleagues on your side when there is a conflict? Do you immediately go on the attack when you are given a nicely intended hint to improve your work?

If you start to heal your inner child, in the long run you will create a better environment at your workplace, get along better with your colleagues and know your limits and hopefully have the courage to express them. Find out why you always enter the boss's office or drive to work on Monday mornings with a sinking feeling in the pit of your stomach. Release these negative thought patterns and lay an important foundation for a healthier and more satisfied professional life.

THE INNER CHILD IN THE SOCIAL ENVIRONMENT

Since the manifestation of childhood pain on past hurts and your learned way of dealing with them can be transferred to all areas of life where we relate to other people or circumstances, you can also apply the method to friendships, social status, family and social structures. Conflicts do not always come out as openly as they do in relationships, and sometimes your emotional reactions may even be a surprise. It can happen, for example, that you are verbally accosted by a complete stranger on the street or in the supermarket and you get so upset about it internally that it keeps you restless for hours afterwards or you still tell your circle of friends about it days later. Furthermore, social, political or economic changes can occur that appeal to your inner child and you react strongly emotionally to them. It is always an expression of how you wish your environment should perceive you, how you perceive your outer world, and what basic need lies behind it. Stay open to the ways your inner child chooses to make itself known.

THE UNHAPPY CHILD AND DIS-EASES

We all strive for well-being and wellness. If needs are not satisfied over a longer period of time, if they are denied and if we permanently expose ourselves to conflicts that burden our psyche, illnesses arise that are the expression of a suffering soul or a suffering body. Neuroses, tinnitus, irritable bowel syndrome, pain disorders, dizziness, eating disorders, depression, burnout, the list is long. To prevent it from getting to this point in the first place, we should learn to focus on ourselves, learn to understand our inner psychological processes and do damage control. Since we all have a shadow child within us, we should try to heal the wounds of the past. Working with the inner child is one of the most important ways to understand yourself and find healing. Your psyche sends you signals through your body and if you do not perceive them, in the worst case, diseases manifest. In other words, your inner child can be sick and give you a hint about it on the physical level.

The severity of an injury you suffer as a child and how you deal with it depends very much on your individual personality structure. If the psychological shock is very strong, it is called a trauma. If the basic needs you had as a child, as mentioned at the beginning, were not fulfilled, if, for example, you were severely neglected, if you experienced physical or verbal abuse or violence, if you received no love at all, it is recommended in any case to seek the help of a trained therapist or to work with a personality coach.

DISEASES AND PRENATAL PROGRAMMING

It is not only the first years of a child's life that are decisive for the inner-psychological processes and the associated behavioral and conflict pattern in later development. Numerous studies investigate the so-called "fetal programming", i.e. the connection between maternal stress during pregnancy and the development of the unborn child.

In the 1980s, the British epidemiologist David Barker laid the foundation for today's research on fetal programming with his observations. He referred to the first study published in scientific circles on Dutch mothers who were pregnant during the winter of 1944/45. The German blockade during World War II led to food shortages and was the trigger for the "Dutch Hunger Winter." Pregnant women were exposed to profound malnutrition and mineral deficiencies at various stages of pregnancy. The "Dutch Famine Birth Chort" study looked at the effects on children born during or shortly after the famine. The children often had lower birth weights and were more likely to develop diabetes, obesity and cardiovascular disease later in life.

A recently published study from McGill University in Canada, under the project name "Ice Storm," investigated the relationship between fetal programming and the child's cognitive and language abilities. It observed 150 children whose mothers were exposed to a 40-day power outage during an ice storm in 1998. Here, a connection between maternal stress and child temperament (hyperactivity), attention deficits, motor and language development deficits was clearly demonstrated.

Mood, existential fears, worries, stress with the partner, unhealthy lifestyle during pregnancy have a great impact on the neural development of the fetus and send facilities to the mental and physical health of the child in the future, responsible for the release of stress hormones such as cortisol or hormonal fluctuations. Altered thyroid hormones in a woman during the first three months of pregnancy, for example, influence the baby's brain development so enormously that an undersupply is associated with an increased risk of developing ADHD or autism.

Scientists suspect that the course for later health or disease is already set at the epigenetic level in the womb. Epigenetics investigates the connection between environmental factors and genetics. The influence of a birth that is as natural as possible on the health of the infant has already been well researched: babies who are born by cesarean section are more likely to suffer from allergies or asthma. Alcohol consumption during pregnancy has shown that the effect in the brain of the unborn child can cause a behavioral disorder and the child itself consumes more alcohol later. A variety of factors could have a prenatal influence, medications, dietary supplements, artificial sweeteners, etc.

If you are one of those people who say that you had an absolutely happy childhood and were met with love and acceptance, yet some emotional blockages or chronic illnesses that are perhaps inexplicable to you turn out to have no clear cause and you can't make any sense of them, then it is worth asking once how your mother felt during and at the beginning of pregnancy. Perhaps you will find a clue here!

Strengthen the happy child

The positive feelings and moods that resided within you when you were little can be harnessed in your life currently and, with a little practice, brought back into your consciousness. Sounds good, doesn't it? In the long run, you'll prevent illness (because a positive attitude strengthens the immune system), boost your self-confidence, access your intuition, feel happiness and joy in life. In short, it's all about having fun!

As a happy child, we are in primal trust and are:

- lighthearted
- playful
- creative

- curious

- cheeky

- spontaneous, impulsive

- happy

- enthusiastic

- full of joy

- completely in the here and now.

It doesn't take much to rekindle these feelings, except that you allow yourself to do it and let it happen. You may feel silly at first, but also realize how good it feels once you start. In the end, you're doing something good for yourself and that's what it's all about. Every coaching, every life advice book, every personal development seminar, every spiritual teaching wants to teach you exactly that! Allow well-being, fulfill your needs, take time for yourself, take care of yourself! In the next chapter you will learn more methods to get in touch with your inner child. For your happy child you should take time regularly.

Here's how to access your happy child:

1. Get creative! Learn a craft or start painting, bake a loaf of bread, rearrange the furniture in your home,

redecorate the rooms, reorganize your closet, do some gardening, plan a party, start model making, set up a workshop, etc. Make something with your hands, shape something, create something, let your imagination run wild!

2. Encourage your playful instinct! (And yes, dear women, don't be so harsh when your partner is watching the soccer game at home with his friends and there is cheering, shouting and suffering! That, too, is the play instinct. Indulge them!) Organize game nights with friends or as a couple, do puzzles, solve puzzles, take the slide at the municipal outdoor pool, participate in escape room games, find the murderer in mystery puzzles, get the old Märklin train set out of the basement, listen to an audio book and follow the action intently. Visit a theme park. Ride a roller coaster! (If that's not possible for you, watch films on the Internet about the highest and steepest roller coasters in the world; the video perspective allows you to be right up front in the first car! This also applies to all other attractions).

3. Be carefree! Dance around the apartment singing your favorite song using a wooden spoon as a microphone, dress colorfully (you don't have to walk around downtown as a bird of paradise), sing out loud in the

shower, take time out for your favorite activity where you completely forget about time, watch fun comedies for a whole day and laugh until your stomach hurts. Plan a night out with your partner or a party where all the guests have to dress up. Hang a hammock on the balcony. Create a trampoline for adults. Let color into your life! Colors have an impact on our mood, so feel free to experiment in your home or clothing choices. This is one of the hardest exercises, because we have forgotten to live in moments without worries, hardships and thoughts of tomorrow.

4. Act impulsively, on a whim. When was the last time you grabbed a popsicle on your way home from the kiosk? It can also be a lick-shell or a ketchup roll! Buy yourself something nice, even if it's not necessary and maybe not budgeted for, because it brings you joy! Go for a walk barefoot in the rain or jump in all the puddles with rubber boots. Get dirty. Plan a spontaneous outing.

5. Feed your curiosity. What has always interested you? Do something or learn something completely new. Try something out. Go to a museum and learn about the past. Read books or magazines. Studies show that curious people are more confident and successful at work, as well as more likely to enjoy going to work.

Curiosity has a positive effect on your memory performance because corresponding areas in the brain are stimulated. Seek contact with strangers, see what happens. Try out the new, eastern Mongolian restaurant. Discover new places and people, travel or discover new destinations. (If travel is not possible at the moment, watch movies on the Internet about places you would like to visit. Learn about other cultures and faraway countries).

6. Make a dream come true! Did you dream of dancing ballet as a child or wanted to have a tree house? Sign up for a "Ballet for Adults" class. It doesn't matter how old you are or what your physical requirements are. It will enhance your coordination and flexibility and yes, I have taken two of these classes myself. Do you have the means to build yourself a treehouse? Maybe just a miniature version for birds? Were you allowed to own a pet as a child? Is there a possibility that you can fulfill this wish today? Animals have a positive influence on our well-being. Find out the small and big dreams and write them down.

7. When was the last time you played a prank on another person and had a good laugh about it? For example, make ugly chestnut figures and give them to

friends and colleagues and enjoy their reaction. Buy a joke item and put it to use!

The possibilities here are unlimited and you may now add to and find out what in particular gives you feelings of happiness. Basically, it's about being completely in touch with yourself, accepting yourself playfully and allowing the little child in us to take up space. For example, you can set aside an hour or two each week to spend time with your sun child.

Getting in touch with the inner child

The first step to bring about a healing of your own inner child is to make contact. Since the emotions of the sun child have more or less general validity, the contact with the shadow child is very individual, since your negative behavioral patterns depend on your very personal experiences.

To make this easier for you, I recommend that you take photos from your early childhood to help you or, if you have them, look at old slides or films. If there are even audio recordings from that time and you still have a tape recorder, listen to the old recordings.

PHOTO EXERCISE

Look at your photos and what facial expression you had at the captured moment. Do you perhaps remember on what occasion the photo was taken? Do you look scared, worried or angry, did you perhaps cry? In the position of a loving adult, talk to the young child in the photo. Ask it what it is feeling, why it is sad or afraid. Ask him what he needs at that moment, how to help him. Tell him that he is safe and in good hands, that he is beautiful and that you love him. Whatever wish you have at this moment, whatever you want to tell your inner child, do it.

DAILY CONVERSATIONS WITH YOUR LITTLE ME

Ask the child in you every day how it is doing and what it needs at the moment. For example, if you look in the mirror after getting up and regularly address the little child in you, with a little practice you will soon get interesting answers. You can also look at a framed photo of yourself, which has a fixed place, and ask it every morning in a recurring ritual. Maybe the little squirt in you says he wants to play today, or the little diva wants something especially nice and colorful. The little me might want to go to Aunt Inge's or spend time with his father. Or it says without further ado: Leave me alone! Here your interpretation ability is now called for and creativity, how you can fulfill the wish - even if only rudimentarily or vicariously. It could look like this: you might get off work a little earlier, devote yourself to your hobby, treat yourself to some-thing nice, talk to a relative on the phone, or drop by your parents' house unannounced to spend some time together.

If your loved one is unfortunately unalive any-more, visiting their final resting place also counts. Per-haps bring a beautiful plant or other object and have loving conversations with the deceased. If your inner child wants to be left alone, it is advisable to comply and schedule important appointments or errands for another day, if possible. You will find that over time this exercise is very healing as you learn mindfulness in dealing with yourself and your needs.

LETTERS TO YOUR INNER CHILD

If you find verbal communication difficult, it is a good idea to write letters to your inner child. Over time, this can develop into an exchange of letters, as your inner child will respond to you. Since the messages are written down, you can serve as an aid to healing if you are not quite sure which negative experience is behind which soul scar. You can start in general or ask specific questions. For example, you might ask when the inner child was sad and if it can describe a situation to you. My inner child once answered me, "Do you remember when I built a cave in the hall closet? It was so really cozy and cozy, I had a flashlight and even Dad's old little radio. I found it so cozy, I would have loved to share that feeling because I was alone. I asked Mom if she would join me in the den, but she just said very maturely and busily that she didn't have time because she had to prepare lunch. This made me abruptly deeply sad that she can't experience this beautiful feeling too, and I then immediately left the cave and dismantled it. Since I notice tears welling up inside me as I write, I want to prepare you for the fact that strong emotions can come up when working with the inner child and please be prepared if tears flow here and there.

CREATE A NOTEBOOK

Here you should separate the pages or chapters between the laughing sun child and the crying shadow child. Stick in pictures of yourself laughing and looking glum. Everything that arises within you, in thoughts, feelings or images during the work with the inner child should be noted in this book.

To track the happy child, you can note the following things:

Do you remember what you loved to play as a child? Who did you play with in the yard and who played which role? Were you more of a cop than a robber? What did you spend the most time doing? What was your favorite toy? What did you laugh the loudest at? What qualities did you like most about your brother/sister? Who did you tell a secret to?

Everything that made you happy as a child, you can write down here. Write down a happy event and what you thought was so great at the time: Summer vacation on the farm was great! We children could play all day and move freely on the grounds, mom and dad have ...

Think back to your inner child's birthday, for example. As children, we usually get special attention on our birthdays, we are little kings for a day, we get great gifts, we get to invite friends, we get to play special games, and we look forward to that day weeks in advance. Write down what made this day so special. How did it make you feel? As an adult, what would the perfect day look like for you to feel that way again? To track the unhappy child, you can write down the following things:

Write down situations or incidents when you were particularly angry, sad, disappointed, or hurt. Was there anything that frightened you terribly? Example: When mom and dad went out or somewhere with my brother, I wasn't allowed to go, I had to stay home. Healing can already begin by identifying and writing down, as an adult today, the little child's message behind it: "You don't belong." Transform it by addressing the little child, "You belong. You weren't allowed to go because Aunt Inge had gotten a new dog from the shelter and it was very aggressive. Mom and Dad were worried and thought it was not a safe environment for a toddler. You are not alone, I am with you."

For example, you can also start the following sentences and complete them yourself:

> • My inner child likes honesty. Always be honest with myself...
>
> • My inner child may be authentic. When have I pretended or fibbed?
>
> • My inner child does not like to obey. When did I always have to obey?
>
> • My inner child does not like punishment. When was I punished and how?
>
> • My inner child does not like to be alone. When did I feel alone and lonely?
>
> • My inner child may be feeling unaccepted. Who has never liked me?
>
> • When was mom mad at me?
>
> • When was dad angry with me?
>
> • What was very mean of my brother/sister?

WORK WITH SYMBOLS

To enter into a dialogue with your inner child, you can hold an old doll in your hand, which symbolically stands for the childlike part in you. It also works with two chairs facing each other. One chair stands for your inner child, the other for you as an adult. Now, when you begin to contact your inner child and talk together about negative emotions and their cause, you can take the appropriate seat or hold the doll, depending on which part you are speaking for. Conclude each of these "meetings" with expressing love for the little child inside you and say goodbye to old beliefs that are no longer valid, for example, by writing them down beforehand and throwing them into a container, burning them later or putting them on the hit list in your personal notebook.

Heal the inner child

Healing can begin by saying goodbye to and disempowering old beliefs, convictions and reaction patterns.

1. These must first be recognized and identified.

2. Take a bifurcated perspective. You are an adult and a toddler at the same time.

3. By looking at and examining the situation from all sides from the perspective of an adult who has far more information available, you can resolve the situation by letting the young child know that what they experienced was often not the truth or was only half the truth.

4. As an adult, you recognize the cause behind the hurt and the desire for acceptance, and you can give your inner child what he or she needs, vicariously through the parent. You show your inner child that he is not alone, that you care for him and that everything he needs to be happy is present in you.

5. Do the work of forgiveness! Forgive the people who have caused you unpleasant feelings. You will thus free yourself from the role of victim and stop holding grudges. The situation itself cannot be undone, but you will learn to deal with the consequences much better.

Whether you prefer terms like "integration of the shadow ego" or "blockage solution" instead of "healing of the inner child" is up to you, the underlying principle is always the same. I would now like to introduce you to ways in which you can heal your inner child. In the previous chapter on establishing contact, you have already learned ways to recognize conflicts and negative experiences from childhood and to identify the resulting negative emotions. Since the transitions in the work are fluid, a healing effect can already begin when contact is made with the inner child and the methods described are applied.

POSITIVE REFORMULATION

Make a list of negative beliefs and rephrase them in positive ways.

Examples:

> •I am ugly. I may not conform to the common ideal of beauty, but I have other unique qualities. I am good the way I am.
>
> •I won't be able to do it anyway. If I put my mind to it, I can do anything I want.
>
> •I don't deserve to be successful and happy. I deserve to be successful and happy.
>
> •I am weak and helpless and cannot change anything. I am strong and can change everything if I want to.
>
> •Nobody loves me. I am lovable and there are people who see it the same way.
>
> •I am not good enough. I am perfectly sufficient, even if I am not perfect, no one is.
>
> •I will never be successful. I am capable of learning and have many skills that I can use profitably.

AFFIRMATIONS

Affirmations are positively formulated beliefs that are called to mind through constant repetition in order to change behavior and beliefs. Affirmations are a tool from autosuggestion. With this method, you will only see success if you constantly stay on the ball. Humans are creatures of habit and with patience and consistency you can reprogram your subconscious mind with affirmations. In the long run, you will learn to evaluate situations more positively with this method. According to a 2015 study, positive affirmations in the brain activate the reward center and the area for self-reflection more strongly. These areas were particularly strongly addressed when the affirmations were formulated purposefully for the future, this was proven by MRI images.

You can recite affirmations out loud, write them down, address them to your reflection, or listen to them.

Examples:

> • I love and appreciate myself with everything that makes me.
>
> • Love fills me.
>
> • I am always in the right place at the right time.

- I am strong and brave.
- I am self-confident and know my strengths.
- My weaknesses are also endearing.
- I respect myself and my body.
- I trust my abilities.
- I take responsibility for myself.
- I deserve to be happy.
- I deserve to be loved.
- I have so much to give to another person.
- Every day I get closer to my goal.

VISUALIZE

Visualization here means an introspection, a day-dream that you construct and direct yourself. Unlike meditation, you don't have to go into deep relaxation. Provide a safe and comfortable atmosphere in which you feel at ease. Close your eyes. In front of your inner eye you can now meet your inner child. Either meet it in a beautiful place where you have always loved to play, for example, or create an imaginary safe space. For example, you could go down a flight of stairs and at the bottom of the steps your inner child is waiting for you. Ask it how it is doing, what it needs to be happy. If you feel that it is sad, comfort it by giving it a hug or words of encouragement. If you have already identified a situation in which your inner child experienced an injury on the part of the parents, you can replay this situation in your mind's eye. Ask your inner child how he experienced this situation and what he felt. Tell it that it was not the complete truth, because the parents acted out of their own insecurity, were perhaps helpless and overwhelmed themselves, or were under a lot of stress. Comfort it by telling it that you will take care of it, love it, and give it what it needs. Ask your inner child if it is ready to forgive the parents. You can then do this together.

MEDITATION

If you have difficulty with visualization, a guided journey to your inner child has a great advantage because you are guided and experience an introduction at the beginning to calm down mentally, to concentrate and to relax physically and mentally. Usually a meditation begins with breathing and mindfulness exercises and you are given a setting in which to mentally go. Your attention is directed to different areas of the body to consciously relax them. Within the meditation you will be guided to your inner child and given space to allow negative emotions to arise and transform them into positive ones or let them go.

Guided meditations are also used by therapists and offered as audio files or CDs by them in the trade. Scientifically, the positive effects of meditation have been flawlessly proven for a long time, and if you incorporate this method into your work with your inner child, you will see noticeable effects after just a few hours: inner peace and balance, stress no longer upsets you so quickly. This in turn has a positive effect on your cardiovascular system, immune system and cholesterol levels.

HYPNOSIS

Hypnosis, which should only be performed by certified therapists, is the art of taking another person's visual, physical and emotional imagination into the past or an alternate reality to experience events. In doing so, the hypnotist will place the person in an altered state of consciousness, the hypnotic trance. In the trance, there is access into the subconscious mind.

The hypnotized person is awake and alert at all times, at the same time deeply relaxed and able to communicate verbally at any time. In a preliminary conversation - if not in the course of behavioral therapy - you will discuss with your therapist situations in which you experienced injuries or negative emotions as a child. In regression, you will experience this situation again - from the perspective of the five-year-old child and "live." Even your voice will change during the hypnosis session and you will speak in the voice of the five-year-old child. Your adult consciousness is by no means turned off, it is watching the entire scene and can be addressed by the therapist as well. With therapeutic guidance, these negatively experienced feelings will be transformed, released and accepted and resolved with the help of the observing adult consciousness.

Limits in the work with the inner child

The confrontation with the inner child should not be understood as a free pass to always and always want to satisfy one's inner child. This concept is also in no way suitable as a justification for expecting something from the social environment. There is a danger of wanting to demand something from the other person because the inner child wants it that way. Especially in a relationship, more problems then arise than one originally wanted to solve.

If you make the mistake and put your inner child in the first place to want to achieve something, then you have skipped the integration into your current reflective adult consciousness a little. Because from the inner child, the ego grows up later!

Embrace dealing with past hurts with a healthy and balanced sensitivity. This is not about a vendetta or belated recriminations. That would be counterproductive and won't get you any further. Develop yourself further and make peace, become happier and more content as a result. I wish this for you from the bottom of my heart!